The Greatest Secrets of the Mystical Laws of Success

A Parabolic Guide to the Secret Habits and Spiritual Strategies of Highly Effective Successful People

By: George S Mentz

I0492609

First published by
Mentzinger Media, LTD
http://www.gmentz.com
Endorsed by the Academy http://www.gafm.com
© George Mentz 2020
The right of George Mentz to be identified as the author of this work has been asserted in accordance with the Copyright, Designs and Patents Act 1988.
ISBN – Disclosed on Publishing
Library of Congress Cataloguing-in-Publication Data
Cataloguing in Publication Data
A catalogue record for this book is available online

Summary of Ideas – A Parabolic Workbook to Success

Table of Contents

The Greatest Secrets of the Mystical Laws of Success 1

Introduction...4

Maximizing The Inner Power – The New Philosophy 6

The Power of Parabolic Thinking 14

Workbook Exercises: 15

Exercise – We Must Act "As If" in Mind and Action..15

Create present Tense Affirmations for All parts of Your Consciousness 16

    Here are examples of affirmations directed at different parts of the SELF. 17

Ask Yourself the Right Questions so that you can Activate Your Deeper Abilities..........18

Find Out What Needs to Go! 19

Authenticity – Be True to Yourself..20

The Stimulus – The Causation of Success 21

Serendipity and Synchronicity 22

The Spirit of The Universe 23

Self Empowerment – For Work and Creativity 24

Take Ownership:..26

Learn as much as you can about 26

Here's a list of the 12 Secret Powers of Achievement..27

You can do it. The 21st Century Effeciencies 29

Laws of Mastery...30

The Framework of Wealth – The Steps to Success 32

How to Get What You Want – Super Charge Your Mind..37

Quotes on Prosperity and Abundance 44

Other References or Authors of Interest..51

Preface - After visiting and meeting with leaders in over 40 nations including executives, Kings, Ambassadors, Barons, Dukes, Spiritual Leaders for various faiths, we have gathered some of the greatest insights to success, happiness, health and prosperity known to the world.

Summary of Ideas – A Parabolic Workbook to Success

Introduction

When discussing the greatest philosophers and psychologists, it is hard to miss their emphasis on human potential and human performance. Top thinkers of the past put a focus on character, thinking, habits, and skills, but they also focus on the use of the consciousness. With the great Ralph Waldo Emerson, he suggested in his writings that fortune is the fruit of your character, and the great Descartes mused over how mankind is equipped to rule over nature and be creative in a way that expresses excellence. From the Stoics to Jeremy Bentham, great thinkers have stated that minimizing struggle is a key objective in maximizing pleasure and success.

According to Schopenhauer, the phenomenal world is not so chaotic but rather operates according to sufficient reason. Schopenhauer implies that the immutable laws of the universe operate with causality or "cause and effect.' Schopenhauer also sees willpower as a kind of force that is always seeking higher expression that strives to not only survive but to grow. With great minds like Dr. Victor Frankl, he espoused that life always has meaning even if that meaning or purpose is not clear at the time. Frankl believed that each person comes into life with unique potentialities to fulfill. To make it more personal, my father, Judge/Sgt. Henry Mentz, believed that his purpose or meaning for his platoon was to win the war in Europe, liberate the people, and free the starving concentration camp survivors such as Dr. Victor Frankl.

Some might say that Freud depicted humans as creatures driven by subconscious carnal urges, but Freud seems to have failed to see the difference between the soul ego compared to the lower ego of instinct. Beyond Freud's focus on instincts, the true secret is to connect to the soul-ego which can assist in maximizing creativity, success, and happiness. Transcending the carnal ego and harnessing its powers is yet another feat of champions and leaders who possess the highest charisma and enthusiasm for leadership.

Dr. William James, the father of modern psychology believed that if we can minimize the gap between our potential and our self actualization, we will have a higher self-regard. Similarly, Carl Jung, who is the godfather of spiritual awakenings believed that Individuation is becoming what you always were meant to be [*potentia* (Latin)] where you fulfill your unique purpose. Dr. Jung famously said, "Spiritus contra spiritum" which literally translates to "spirit against spirit". Loosely translated, it refers to "a spiritual experience is the only way to counter a deadly affliction of the spirit such as addiction.

As with Spinoza, Einstein seemed to agree that the universe is governed by impersonal natural laws where Einstein actually said, "I believe in Spinoza's God". Einstein probably means that there is substance in all things that may be unseen such as quantum physics, but if you realize how to cooperate with the impersonal laws of your environment, you can and will prosper at a higher level than others. There are various laws that we take for granted such as the laws of electricity, thermodynamics, aerodynamics, motion, principle of least resistance, and so forth. For instance, the path of least resistance is the physical or metaphorical pathway that provides the least resistance to forward motion by a given object or entity, among a set of alternative paths. With the use of the mind and action, there are various ways to cooperate, engage, or avoid people places and things. To engage learning, to avoid dangerous situations, to maximize strength in body, mind and spirit are all ways to lead a more efficient and effective lifestyle. However, you can do many things right, but if you do one thing incessantly wrong, you can blow up your life also. I have seen celebrities, rock stars, royalty, and millionaires lose everything to drugs and addictions while also going to the gym, doing yoga and attending church each week. So, the moral of the story is to maximize constructive behavior and stay clear of destructive things. Get a plan and use methods and activities to expand your life, love, and friendships.

Maximizing The Inner Power – The New Philosophy

I remember being at the Yale Club of New York City years ago researching philosophy and metaphysics and doing research at the nearby New York Library and the Yale Club Library.

While comparing many great gurus for the history of the world I came to a simple conclusion. From Buddha to Jesus, from Kant to Hegel, from Marcus Aurelius to Benjamin Franklin, the common denominator is subjective but the same and that is, "The great thinkers all seek peace of mind". Most wise folks know that with peace, you have a greater awareness, a clean running computer, less attachments, and the person "at peace" is free with expansive thinking and creativity.

As some point, all of us develop an internal hunger for a higher purpose and to master our destiny during our lives. This instinctive fire in the belly seemingly compels us to think and take action; we must change and adapt. Growth is necessary for the human condition. Finding a reason for being, where we can cultivate our talents and use them to improve life for ourselves and those we love, becomes vitally important. Striving for the personal best in ourselves while serving humanity is an ideal both important and noble. It is part of our desire for a greater good. Becoming the best we can be and doing the things we love to do in service and in leisure is a natural desire. This is true whether one is a righteous member if any religion or a follower of a philosophical practices, virtues, and ethics. The state of Abundance is possible when we inherently understand the need to adapt, grow, and be prepared. You hold the golden key when you master your destiny by improving yourself in mind body and spirit.

This codex is a summary of the key philosophy and secrets needed to advance to your highest potential. If you need to learn even more to prepare yourself for this guide, we suggest several other authors: Marcus Aurelius, the gospels of Jesus Christ,

Buddha, Pythagoras, Hegel, Kant, Emerson, von Goethe, Meister Eckhart, poetic Vedas and Eddas, the Book of Psalms, Zoroaster, Lao Tzu, Socrates, Plato, Aristotle, the Upanishads, and any great wisdom literature. Then, of course, we can seek more light from the authors in the bibliography.

One of the greatest secrets of mankind is that leaders and professionals have quietly used the philosophy contained herein for centuries. Keep this book close, use this secret technology, and master your destiny.

Whatever our vocation may be (e.g., mechanic or artist), you will need the right instruction and tools to gain excellence. The importance of natural expression is absolutely necessary for personal accomplishment and prosperity. Your highest form of expression requires an imaginative and resourceful life; it involves the abundance of ideas, things, and actions.

True and lasting prosperity has a spiritual foundation and balance. Genuine success is mastering excellence in body, mind, and spirit. When there is balance, ideas and energy naturally come from the universe to the person who is exercising this higher order of existence. When we are at our best and acting as effective individuals, we actually have more insights flowing to us from the universal source or consciousness of the infinite.

No let us focus firstly on the great philosophers of science and ethics. These great thinkers all contribute different ingredients to the recipe of a rich and fuller life. Read what each of them has to say, ponder their ideas, and then you will be ready to examine the rest of the book.

- Rene Descartes simplifies the essence of philosophy: "I think, therefore I am." With this statement, we must be able to find our being, or what people call their being-ness.

The key is to reconnect your spirit and deeper-self with the universe in a way that is harmonious.

- George W. F. Hegel, a German philosopher, also believed that reality was absolute Spirit; we participate in our destinies and create our own realities.

- Meister Eckhart, the fourteenth-century Christian Neo-Platonist, personified the spiritual basics in these words "If the only prayer you say in your life is 'Thank You,' that would suffice."

- Socrates said, "Know thyself," and, "The unexamined life is not worth living." Be willing to take a hard look at yourself in the mirror, and seek an honest appraisal of your character and behavior and let go.

- The French existentialist Jean-Paul Sartre was clear about accountability. We should start having responsibility for our actions going forward and refuse to be bogged down with self-victimization and blame. We must deal with the past.

- Ben Franklin, in his autobiography, used a process called the precept of order, where each day he took time to review his day, set goals, and see where he could improve his actions and character.

- Nietzsche said, "That which does not kill us makes us stronger," Thus, we need to face fear and get out of our comfort zones.

- Marcus Aurelius so eloquently said, "Take full account of the excellencies which you possess, and in gratitude remember how you would hanker after them, if you had them not." Aurelius includes another great quote that we should follow: "It is not death that a man should fear, but he should fear never beginning to live."

- Humanistic psychologists Carl Rogers and Abraham Maslow believed that people have an innate drive to be all they can be and to self-actualize. This intrinsic metaphysics plays a large role in facilitating the progression of the best in each of us.

- Aristotle's theory of potentiality: "Within each of us is a natural evolution toward fulfilling our potential."

- Immanuel Kant has implied that OUR Perception IS our reality. If you focus your thoughts on the best, then you will attract the best. Feed yourself with things that are good, learning about what is excellent, and these things will build your worldview and character.

- Dr. Carl Jung theorized that one finds their natural talents deep within the spirit of one's self. When we get in touch with our natural inclinations, it elevates our outward expression. It may not be easy, but if you act toward your higher purpose each day, the cosmic momentum will build to your advantage.

- Both Aristotle and Thomas Aquinas refer to God as the 'First Cause" or "Pure Mind." In essence, we come from this pure mind and first cause; we are created from the Source. We have desires and ideas flowing to us from a higher source at all times. What you do with your ideas and imagination is of extreme importance. Your ideas are yours, they are priceless, and they are consciously coming to you in every moment. Your creativity is your abundance

- The poet Johann Wolfgang von Goethe famously stated that "boldness is genius."

- Acclaimed self help author Robert Collier also believed that beginning any task created a nucleus of activity, bringing form from the formless. If you begin something and maintain faith in the process, you may then utilize the act of gratitude and praise which is like watering a flower with nourishment. In the same way a flower needs water, the universe craves peace, thanks, praise, and action, and the universe will respond accordingly with blessings.

- Engels and Marx believed firmly in productivity as the key to progress. The big metaphysical secret lies in becoming one with your desires, because you then become in tune with your objective! When we blend purpose and spirituality, our energy then becomes laser focused.

- The philosopher of existentialism Soren Kierkegaard was famous for saying, "We must think for ourselves and be suspicious of groupthink, and we should not worry about the ignorance of neighbors and society."

- Remember, Emerson, St. Augustine, and Plato believed that evil is not a diabolical force but rather the absence of good.

- Henry David Thoreau believed that we should put our "Conscience before conformity." Thus, your natural creativity and labor will be fun, and you will learn to freely accept premiums and rewards for your quality services and the products in relation to your craft.

- British political philosopher John Locke believed in a liberal, anti-authoritarian theory of the state. His practical theory of knowledge advocated religious toleration and personal identity. His philosophy suggests that order is necessary to protect the individual, and man is endowed with inalienable rights where these rights are gained through work and effort.

- Alfred Wallace, the founder of evolution theory with Darwin, systematically came to believe evolution was sometimes guided by a higher power and that evolution could not account for the evolution of consciousness.

- The nineteenth-century European philosopher Arthur Schopenhauer believed that we are motivated by our will, and it is our will that is our sense of reality. Therefore, willingness is at the core of our growth and advancement. Desire is good and comes from the Spirit. Seeing past the illusion of what seems apparent, and acting on healthy desires, is the key to growth and happiness.

Whether you are a student of Locke, Emerson, Ayn Rand, Ben Franklin, Frederick Douglas, or Buddha, there are some eternal truths. The great lesson from many of the world's legendary philosophers is that the individual is an important and unique part of the whole. Each person should master themselves; education, knowledge, and inner peace are essential. Efficient effort is vital for advancement. Growing in faith, knowingness, and wisdom are all important factors of duty to ourselves and to society. Your contributions may seem small, but your spiritual creativity and service may positively affect generations to come. Overall, the ripple effect of one pebble tossed in the lake has a broad impact on the whole of its contents.

The results of practicing these principles and suggestions will result in a natural expression of your life purpose that becomes a reality—you will become who you were meant to be. It may require great energy from you, but it will feel eventually like child's play. You may find many challenges, but the experience of life will be invigorating when you pause in those moments to stop and smell the roses. Life is delicate and sometimes short, and you may be compelled to dedicate energy to definitive ends. All mortals are faced with these timeless questions: What do you want to be remembered for? How do you want to impact the world? What is your potential legacy?

You have within you the power to connect to the universal force. This force is the creative and animating energy that permeates the universe. Like gravity or electricity, the Force is not seen, but exists as the all-pervading framework for which every law hinges upon. This interstellar force is also known as God or "The Life Force". This unlimited power is everywhere as creation is constant. New ideas, new art & music, new planets, new galaxies, new species, new worlds are continuously manifesting at this very moment.

That special part of your consciousness that can be in-tune with this force is referred to by the great teachers of metaphysics as the subjective mind or higher consciousness.

Directed thought-energy can be focused where the individual may act as a creative force within the universal framework. This supernatural power is willing to serve you and grant you anything that you earnestly and sincerely desire with focus, action, heartfelt gratitude and emotion.

If Faith is the substance of things hoped for, then that very Substance can also be qualified as the energy of our attention and thoughts. Belief and faith are the same in that they mean that we accept what is unseen. Energy is consciousness, and thus, "thought awareness" is energy. All things created equally in perfect balance, the energy of faith, attention, and mind can tilt the cosmic balance of life, happiness, and success in our favor.

'his is why spiritual-metaphysics is so important because the)articipant who engages mental-cooperation with universal law ittains the ability to optimize: body, mind and spirit. The galactic ramework of forces that we seek to cooperate with is what many :all: "the Spirit of the Universe" and "the spirit within you".

\ll of us go through life with a steady stream of ideas, thoughts, ind desires. Tapping into that greater, infinite-self expands our ntuitive abilities to best use our priceless inspiration. Thus,)ecoming aware that we may operate at a higher order of being is vhere achievement truly begins, and then, we become willing to ake the actions that provide results. Co-operation with the "force of the universe" and the framework of the metaphysical laws that iffect mankind is the path to maximize our existence, :ontributions, and consciousness.

.earning to use the mind and concentrate on our desires is where ;elf actualization begins. Even the great Marconi was referred to the nsane-asylum by government officials for suggesting that nformation and thoughts can be sent over the airwaves. However, oday all of us know that we can tune into any given channel and send messages millions of miles. Harnessing the power of prayer, neditation and contemplation is where inspiration and well-being is :ultivated. With this power of mental focus and cooperation with he universal law, we become masters of our destiny.

From Taoism to Christianity, and from Eastern and Western :ultures, the mystics believed in a timeless and formless force that ;overns the cosmos. Most of the founding fathers of the United States were deists who believed in the Source or a supreme God. We ire born of this cosmic force, and we have the ability to more ;ffectively cooperate as spiritual and physical beings in conjunction vith this force. Listen to your heart and allow yourself to become ind evolve into your highest expression; get in tune with the world ind allow yourself to manifest your Quantum Bliss....

The Power of Parabolic Thinking

1. The quality of your dominant thoughts is the causative and chief creative factor that produces success in all cases.
2. Cultivating the ability to withdraw attention from what is not useful in our life, is a great power.
3. Use your thought and mind to build worth and value into your life. Worth and character is built though abilities, performance, skills, mental perception, and results.
4. We must seek the experiences we want in our lives.
5. We must learn what those experiences we seek "would be like" so that we can sense and feel their manifestation in our minds eye.
6. We can maximize our imaginative abilities be practicing the art of seeing the future desired results in our minds eye.
7. We must remove the thoughts that don't serve us. Put recurring negative thoughts into a box, fasten it, and burn the box in your imagination, and send box or smoke away and release it permanently.
8. Decide that we will strive to avoid the same mistakes of the past. Past mistakes are sometimes priceless as we know how to navigate the obstacles when we try again.
9. What influences to we want in our life. News, Views, Friends, etc. What type of learning do you want? What type of exercise or strengthening activities do you want?
10. What kinds of joys, peace and thoughts do you want to have?

Workbook Exercises:

Exercise – We Must Act "As If" in Mind and Action

1. Write things out that you want to be/do/have
2. Imagine these ideas being imprinted in & on your picture screen of subconscious mind.
3. Picture your fulfilled desires in your deeper mind as a fact and memory.
4. Feel the joy and aliveness of attainment of all you seek.
5. Repeat several days a week. Carry the list on paper with you.
6. Focus on your chief aims & primary intentions which will cause mind to disclose ideas & pathways for your success.
7. Act as if the life you seek is yours now. Be that person
8. Imagine a bright golden circle of protection and projection that radiates around you and protects your home and family. This golden circle of protection projects your successful energy of your future life.

Write out a few things that you want to have in your life:

1) _____

2) _____

3) _____

4) _____

5) _____

Create present Tense Affirmations for All parts of Your Consciousness

1. Affirmations are speaking to your own consciousness either mentally or out loud. You can write affirmations out and read them to yourself or memorize them and say them to yourself.
2. You can handcraft Affirmations for yourself.
3. Write Affirmations out where you imagine the qualities of value that you want to have.
4. Imagine having all of these attributes such as strength, confidence, memory, confidence, poise, importance, value/worth, faith, skill, loving nature, academic abilities and more.
5. Imagine all of the great attributes surrounding you like an aura and radiating from your body and mind all the time.
6. Affirmations can be done by applying an affirmation to specific parts of your mindset.
7. When you instill yourself with affirmations, qualities, and a mindset of success, people begin to sense your energy.
8. Example: My health is excellent and every cell in my body is renewed each day, my mind and memory are excellent.

Write out a few Affirmations here:

1)_____

2) _____

3) _____

4) _____

5) _____

Here are examples of affirmations directed at different parts of the SELF.

- I AM wealthy healthy and happy
- My soul and spirit are happy healthy and wealthy
- My deeper consciousness accepts that I am healthy and wealthy and happy
- My mind and memory are powerful and my mind remembers all necessary information.
- My heart, lungs, and organs are strong, vibrant and potent.
- From my head to my toes, my body and energy is strong, young, and full of endurance.
- My skin, aura, and body is healthy, vibrant, and strong.
- My perception and mental abilities are powerful and responsive.
- My mental, physical and spiritual health is wonderful and every cell of my body is renewed and energized every day.

Ask Yourself the Right Questions so that you can Activate Your Deeper Abilities

If we have not achieved success, many times we are not receiving what we seek because we have not looked at the right questions. We must ask ourselves the correct questions to allow the mind and memory and soul to absorb, comprehend, sense & feel the questions while working on the answers, and solutions to your challenges and your desires.

1. What would I like to have?
2. What would I like to be?
3. What would I like to do?
4. Where would like to go?
5. What would I like to create?
6. What do I want to look like.

If you don't have answers to these questions, you may just need more specificity in your life. We need to cultivate and develop priorities and options so that you may better be aligned with your destiny.

Write out jobs or things or successes that you would like to achieve/obtain.

1)_____

2) _____

3) _____

4) _____

5) _____

Find Out What Needs to Go!

1. Make a list of things that are not necessary in your life
2. Begin to "let go of" or avoid these unnecessary things or get rid of the habits, people, places or things that hold you back.
3. Find other healthy habits to replace what you have "let go of".
4. The ability to unravel conscious snags gives great power. Itemizing and discovering the obstacles that hinder you is important
5. Once itemized, then you can begin to create the intent to remove non-productive behavior and relationships.
6. Deep thinking about getting rid of dead weight and bad habits is a great start. This technically cultivates intent.
7. Mental obstacles are often great barriers to success, but many of them can be removed or even transformed.
8. Learning how to remove mental obstacles and eliminating deeper consciousness obstacles can give great power

Write out great habits that you can engage to replace old habits.

1) _____

2) _____

3) _____

4) _____

5) _____

Authenticity – Be True to Yourself

Being authentic about who you are & what you do gives you great enthusiasm and great creative ability

1. We don't have to be who our parents were. You need not have their job, profession, attitude, or life consequences.
2. You don't need to be what your brothers and sisters are in life. Whether they are doctors, teachers, or other, you don't need to be like them or compete with them.
3. You can break the Chain and become who you were meant to be. If bad things happened to you as a young person during your upbringing, you need not continue that way of thinking or acting of others in your family.
4. Write out who you think you should be by describing your future self, and describe those amazing characteristics that you seek. Imagine yourself being that what you seek "in the NOW".

Write out traits of our most authentic self.

1)_____

2) _____

3) _____

4) _____

5) _____

The Stimulus – The Causation of Success

Motivation and Stimuli - We all know that every person has unique stimuli which motivates them to go great lengths to obtain what they seek. Therefore energy always follows your focus but sometimes to create focus we need some sort of stimuli. To create stimuli, investigate the various powers of your primary motivational desires.

Try to APPEAL to your primary motivations

1. Appeal to the power survival
2. Appeal to the power of passion
3. Appeal to the power of love
4. Appeals of the power of prestige
5. Appeal to the power of Hunger and creativity

If we can appeal to our greater desires, our dreams may outweigh the other distractions and habits that have been holding us back.

Write out what stimulates your desire to improve your life?

1) _____

2) _____

3) _____

4) _____

5) _____

Serendipity and Synchronicity

Learn to act upon fate – Serendipity is the connecting principle that links mind to matter.

1. Learn to be still and open your heart and mind to the flow of ideas and inspiration from the universe.
2. Write down your great ideas.
3. Write down the tasks that are required to make these great ideas a reality.
4. Learn to be able to notice patterns in your life. Try to perceive the signs or symbols that enhance or confirm your opinions.
5. Learn to use inspiration. Learn to call that person or e-mail at person. When the thought to ask for help or insight comes to you, send that message out into the person. As long as the message does no harm, seeking to expand your life and relationships is good. Inspiration to connect to others works in mysterious ways.

Write out some ideas and patterns that you have had lately? This may be the universe guiding you to something.

1)_____

2) _____

3) _____

4) _____

5) _____

The Spirit of The Universe

Why is The Spirit of the Universe important? God is the framework and the energy that binds the universe together. Learning to act in concert with the power of the universe gives us a great advantages and powers.

1. With awareness and focus, we can pay attention to our experiences.
2. We must learn to act and live towards the realization of our vision & learn how to use our willingness "as a power".
3. We must have resilience to be able to navigate challenges.
4. We must have alignment and make sure that our work is not going against our dreams. Do the results you are seeking look like a good-ethical and spiritual fit for you?.
5. Intentions are important. With empowering our intentions, we must maintain certain thinking and maintain certain actions which create a stimuli and catalysts to create what we seek.

Self Empowerment – For Work and Creativity

1. Make lists of your personality and character assets.
2. What products and services to you like the most and believe in?
3. It may be best to take a job with a company that has products and services we believe in.
4. Or start a company that creates products and services that you believe in strongly.
5. What is your purpose? An example of a purpose is "helping others have a better life in the areas of wealth health and happiness.
6. What are your core values?
7. We should be able to work and create in areas that do not conflict with our values

Satisfaction List - Do something that you want to do. Do you like to ?

a) Travel
b) Teach
c) Play music or listen to music
d) Create web sites are pictures
e) Write stories or essays
f) Speaking or acting

What can you do in these areas to enjoy life and make money

If you need education licenses; then, do the research and engage the learning that you need to master your destiny.

Write out some things you want to do, see, or new skill or new hobby.

1) _____

2) _____

3) _____

4) _____

5) _____

Take Ownership:

Take ownership of Your Destiny which includes your:

1. Life
2. Work
3. Dream
4. Speech
5. Thought
6. Body
7. Mind
8. Soul

Write out a list of 5 things & you will take ownership of.

1) _____

2) _____

3) _____

4) _____

5) _____

Learn as much as you can about

1. Yourself
2. Dreams
3. Goals
4. Job
5. School
6. Business
7. Or Do research on nights and weekends.
8. How you fit into the workforce.

Summary of Ideas – A Parabolic Workbook to Success

Here's a list of the 12 Secret Powers of Achievement

1.   **Desire** – What do you truly and earnestly want to be, do and have.

2.   **Curiosity and Fascination** – What fascinates you? Something that you are passionate about will be both enjoyable and fun while expanding your life.

3.   **Love and Self Respect** – What are you doing to better yourself each day to make you feel good about who you are.

4.   **Wisdom and Knowledge** – What knowledge or skills do you need to maximize your future toward your destiny.

5.   **Inspiration and Intention** – Have you learned to tap into your creative mind? Sit still, and allow thoughts, ideas and solutions to come to you. It takes practice, but the mind is the great creator.

6.   **Analyze** – You must cultivate the awareness and mindset to look at and analyze challenges accurately.

7.   **Planning**- You must create plans or other people will make a plan for you. Planning involves making lists, itemizing tasks, and embedding ideas and goals into your mindset.

8.   **Patience and Persistence** – Are you willing to do what must be done each day to achieve your goals.

9.   **Action and Boldness** – Are you willing to begin and do each day what needs to be done. Each task is a step in the direction toward completion of a goal or group of goals.

10.   **Imagination and Vision** – Can you imagine and see your desired results for each goal you seek with specificity. Space, Size, Color, Sound, Feelings, Emotions, and Visual comprehension of what the completed success looks like?

11.   **Faith and Belief** – Faith is the substance of things unseen. It is belief and energy all wrapped into one unseen power. If you can maintain, focus, and utilize this energy, it will tip the scale of every undertaking in your favor.

12.   **Continuous Improvement and Momentum** – Are you willing to take time each year to better your character, skills, faith, and philosophical life.

Summary of Ideas – A Parabolic Workbook to Success

You can do it. The 21st Century Effeciencies

With the type of technology that we have today with the ability to use computers and the Internet, we have 10 to 100 times greater research power than we did 20 or 30 years ago. You can take free courses online we can read books online for free, you can have books read to you online. You can search for jobs anywhere in the world with the stroke of a few keys.

What is your personality type. Overall you need to figure out whether you want to work for self a small company or large corporation in big organizational chart.

Most people generally speaking have worked for the government or a major corporation or small businesses for a few years before they set out on their own.

By getting work experience, they have learned key skills at these companies discovering how to deal of customers or repair things, learning about products and services.

If we work in a place that interests you, we can learn very much in just six months or in a matter of 2 to 3 years, we can learn a whole lot about how a company works.

Careers are 100% easier to research today. My father who was a Judge and brilliant scholar spent years researching a book that you could assemble and write in a week today. Another friend of my spent several thousand hours on genealogy research of which he could complete in as little as a week today

Thus, the world is vibrant and full of technology to help you.

Laws of Mastery

1. **Laws of Sowing** – Carefully picking the seeds you plant in your consciousness and sub consciousness. Careful sowing will allow the reaping of what you seek rather than weeds and failing crops.

2. **Consequences and Reaping – Receiving –** Receiving is a lost art to many. You must be ready and willing to accept the gift of good fortune with an open hand instead of a closed fist.. Further, you must be able to accept good fortune also by having the correct receptacle for receiving such good will such as bank accounts, value to exchange, services to provide, and so forth.

3. **Laws of Becoming** – You must learn to become that which you seek. If you want to be a successful Wall Street executive, you must become that person in character, skills, and habits.

4. **Law of Adapting and Lessons** – There is a seed of success in every opportunity. Even if you fail, you may later overcome the obstacle though new found knowledge, and lessons learned.

5. **Law of Character** – The law of character is simple but complex. Your character IS based on your thinking, actions and inactions. Learning to control these powers is true mastery.

6. **Law of Imagination, Focus and Imprinting** – Imagination is a skill that is developed. People who can visualize what they want and how they are able to get to it are masters of multi-dimensional chess in their minds.

7. **Law of Flow and Circulation** – There is a Yin and Yang to giving and receiving. We must not suffocate the flow of life force. Money is even a form of energy, and when we bless what we spend and thus expanding our energy flow. We give to people and organizations who either need it or divinely inspire us.

8. **Law of Alchemy and Transmuting** – Like a snake that molts its skin each year, we are constantly changing, growing and transforming. It is possible for us to let go of the old skin and morph into new and higher versions of ourselves. We must be willing to let go of the old and move to the new.

9. **Law of Supply and Ideas** – Substitutes – With every idea is a form of new supply. Some great business successes and authors only began with a single idea. Galaxies and stars seem to be created every year from nothingness. With everything that becomes scarce, something else seems to be created as a substitute. Always remember that creativity is the true raw material of our existence.

10. **The Law of Praxis** – 30 years ago, I never thought that basketball players or tennis players could be much greater than: Byrd, Magic, Borg or McEnroe; however, the field of human performance and praxis/practice seems to keep expanding. If you look at the stats for NBA 3pt shooters for today compared to those of 20 years ago, the changes are significant and stunning. They say that many players today practice 2,000 shots a week. Thus, practices really does make perfect.

The Framework of Wealth – The Steps to Success

1. As beings that desire increasing life, we each contain energies of body, mind and spirit of which we must maintain equilibrium between all three energies. To preserve this balance we utilize our threefold powers. Use of mental, spiritual and physical powers in a spiritual way must produce abundance.
2. All thoughts begin with an idea which is the byproduct of divine connection to the source of all thought.
3. The ideas in back of the thought are the mystical form of all creation and the underpinnings of tangible results or manifestation.
4. All thoughts tend to lead to the field of potential outcomes for all actions, inactions, and creation.
5. Deep Thinking or what is believed in mind habitually becomes who you are and is your essence or character.
6. Free will creates Choices where commitments must be selected. We all have the ability to choose how we use free will in terms of thoughts and actions.
7. Choices create the nucleus of new form and begin a chain reaction if the choice is fueled with emotion and belief.
8. Emotions that fuel manifestation are love, joy, peace, happiness, goodness, and other positive emotions.
9. When each idea is transformed into a intention, then each intention may be transformed into a plan, vision, and mission. Then it is chosen as a prime objective for the individual
10. When the plan is primus it becomes a purpose which is backed by belief.
11. When firm belief, earnestness and constructive emotion are in back of a purpose, it is energized.
12. Our belief system must be based on the constant and creative possibility of optimal results and prosperity.

Everyone who is living upright in a spiritual way is deserving and capable of tapping into this abundance.

13.   We become best at co-creating our destiny when we are in spiritual unity with the universe where a person develops the realization of the Divine Presence within one's own self.

14.   We operate most effectively when we are awakened and clear in mind. Attunement and forgiveness of ourselves and others allows us to be free of anger and to live in the present moment fully in an awakened state of mind.

15.   Acceptance - We must believe that prosperity and well-being is our birthright.

16.   Believe that you have wealth and freedom and that you are the essence of creative ability.

17.   Everything that is needed is continually provided by an ever expanding world and universe that is abundant and impersonal.

18.   We must understand the essence or rationale behind the purpose of each desire that we want to cultivate.

19.   Further, we must comprehend in some way how our big ideas will help others along with ourselves to convey the sincere impression of value, worth, and increase.

20.   Before implementing each plan or taking any big step, we evaluate our mental effectiveness. Getting clear and going thought a catharsis of mind. This means to look at your track record, atone, prune, purge, and clear away the mental debris. Begin to use "what works" and start to utilize the best practices which make you efficient.

21.   Clear Objectives - Set specific goals, research and refine them. After the purpose, task and objective is clear, then push forward with persistence.

22.   Results Driven.   What is the mission, destination, vision. Develop affirmations that correlate to the most favorable end-result.

23.   Think, feel and act "AS IF" you are already in possession of the life that you want. Cultivate your emotions and your character around the "As If". You must become what you want which means you become the person who owns the life you desire.

24.   Look at where you are, where you are going and periodically reset the course and navigation to optimize the journey.

25.   Learn to think and speak in a prosperous way that conveys peace, abundance, and increase. Mold the habits and tendencies of your thought. Refuse to accept lack and fear.

26.   Take action. Keep lists and do three things toward your dreams per day, do them constructively to the best of your ability.

27.   Study your life, reflect on your day, decide how to continually improve yourself. Do your homework and do all you can to learn and know your purpose, objectives and master your skills. Be the best at what you do and BE Known for your excellence.

28.   Meditations and Prayer - Write out affirmative meditations such as, "Each day I am improving". Write out 10 statements that are affirming and positive. Contemplate over them each day. You can write out generalized affirmations or very specific ones.

29.   Use the affirmative statements or contemplation, to increase acceptance of our potential and boost our awareness.

30.   Visualize - See yourself in optimal circumstances in your mind's eye and Feel it. If you can visualize the optimal result,

then see the next step. Example. See yourself a few pounds leaner toward your optimal weight.

31.   Choose your environment. Select what to feed yourself. Mold your circumstances by your actions and specific thought.

32.   Organize your affairs. Gain the habit of finishing things well. Become excellence, simplify your life, empty the clutter, and redefine your focus. Develop prosperity based routines.

33.   Imprint and affirm your ideals and dreams into your consciousness. The plan, desired thing, or result must be written and then verbalized. It should be claimed into this world using the spoken word.

34.   Make wealth and excellence a priority. Align your thoughts to attract excellence and wealth. Be aware, be open, learn to receive from others, offer praise, and appreciate life. Accept your potentiality, gifts, and abundance.

35.   Circulate your GOOD. Service and Giving - Donate time or money to people or organizations who are the source of your spiritual sustenance.

36.   Sixth Sense - Learn and practice creativity, awareness, and contemplation. Keep a journal, write out ideas, develop and allow a universal flow of inspiration and ideas into your life.

37.   Review and remember your actions. Reflect on what you have done well each day and things you may not have excelled upon. Be determined to be better and do the right thing. Over 200 years ago, Ben Franklin worked his precepts of order each evening. He wanted to be excellent and build his character even at a mature age.

38.   Research ideas - What are your passions, how do your ideas serve? Listen to your intuition & cultivate strategy. Look at what it would take to implement or be successful with your

new ideas: then act on them, implement the plan, review the plan and then improve it.

39.   List out streams of income and potential ways to serve and be prosperous. List how you will expand your life. Go past your comfort zones. List goals beyond your expectations and have deadlines of specificity. You can always change the date.

40.   Review your lists and projects. Check off your accomplishments.

41.   Meet with partners, family and/or spouse to define goals.

42.   Discover your natural expression. What is your labor of love. Where do your passions lie. Remember that you work to pay bills, but you should always follow your dreams. Devote 20 percent of your waking hours each week to your passion. If you become great at it, odds are you can earn a living doing it too.

43.   Character - How do you want to BE.? Self respect and self regard can be developed and nurtured. When you rebuild yourself, you will in-turn love yourself better which allows you to be kinder, more generous, and more loving to others.

44.   With Character comes responsibility toward your mental, physical and spiritual health. Do what works to take care of yourself with: diet, exercise, learning, sleep, study, and fellowship.

45.   Associate with those who can help you where you can also help them. Create a network of business and spiritual friends.

46.   Be good to yourself. Learn health self regard and cultivate a loving relationship with the Source.

47.   Teaching others - Giving it away to keep it.

48.   Law of Increase and Charisma - Radiate abundance, cheer and enthusiasm. Be contagious with love, cheer, and enthusiasm.

How to Get What You Want – Super Charge Your Mind

1. Consciousness & Mind has been described as the substance by which the soul is given the chance to experience existence in the physical world.

2. There is no greater service to humanity than to make the best of yourself.

3. YOU must get rid of the last vestige of the old idea that there is a Deity whose will it is that you should be poor, or whose purposes may be served by keeping you in poverty.

4. In order to know more, do more, and be more we must have more; we must have things to use, for we learn, and do, and become, only by using things. We must get rich, so that we can live more.

5. To get rich, you need only to use your will power upon yourself.

6. Do not talk about poverty; do not investigate it, or concern yourself with it. Never mind what its causes are; you have nothing to do with them.

7. What concerns you is the cure. Use your will power to keep your mind OFF the subject of poverty, and to keep it fixed with faith and purpose ON the vision of what you want.

8. If your heart is set on domestic happiness, remember that love flourishes best where there is refinement, a high level of thought, and freedom from corrupting influences; and these are to be found only where riches are attained by the exercise of creative thought, without strife or rivalry.

9. Getting what you want is in the effective application of a cause

10. The cause of success is always in the person who succeeds

11. The key to success is finding the cause of success and replicating the cause.

12. Use your strongest faculty, and you can cultivate any faculty

13. Can I have to realize you are potential and empower you must use your faculties in your skills effectively

14. You must learn to create conscious action.

15. Cultivate Gratitude and Harmonious Mind

16. Poise is the combination of peace and power that can be applied to each action or thought.

17. Act in a Certain Way in all you do with effectiveness, efficiency and providing value or increase to all.

18. Power consciousness is the secret to success. Power consciousness is what you feel when you know that you can do a thing and you KNOW exactly how to do it.

19.	Belief is the other key to mastery because you MUST believe that it is possible for you to achieve success, while you must believe that you can learn how to do something effectively and flawlessly.

20.	The more steady and continuous your faith and purpose, the more rapidly you will get rich, because you will make only POSITIVE impressions upon Substance; and you will not neutralize or offset them by negative impressions.

21.	The picture of your desires, held with faith and purpose, is taken up by the Formless, and permeates it to great distances-throughout the universe

22.	You must bring things from your conscious mind into your subconscious so that you will know instinctively how to do tasks. Truly knowing in your deeper mind is similar to when you drive a car and speak on the phone as your deeper mind is Knowingly and unconsciously guiding your driving.

23.	We must learn how to effectively send ideas, techniques, and plans from the idea phase in mind into our subconscious mind. We can use tools such as auto suggestion and making a picture board, or use incantations to imprint ideas onto our sub consciousness

24.	Learn to utilize your existing assets in the now

25.	Learn to affect the function of each task you engage

26.	Do all you can in the now and feel your present place in the now

27.   Make use of your present environment

28.   Form of a clear conception of which you see in your mind and on the picture screen of your mind

29.   You can phone clear conceptions of each task that needs to be achieved

30.   Become more successful by using constructively the business you have now

31.   We may secure more friends buy using constructively the network you already have

32.   We may achieve greater domestic happiness by the constructive use of the love that already exists in your home.

33.   You can get what you want in the future by concentrating all your energies upon the constructive use of whatever you are in relation with today and the NOW

34.   A surplus of life causes evolution, growth, and opportunity.

35.   Take an interest in all people you meet me the business of socially and since their leaders of the best for them. This will create the advancement for you

36.   Respect yourself the absolutely charged to all put life into every act and fought and fixed power consciousness fought up on the fact that you are entitled two big promotion it will come as soon as you can more than feel your present place in everyday

37.   Our you must be well rounded and balanced and body and mind and soul and in love.

38.   Focus on doing what must be done. Take action in areas that can be effective in your life.

39.   Whenever you find yourself hurrying, call a halt; fix your attention on the mental image of the thing you want, and begin to give thanks that you are getting it. The exercise of GRATITUDE will never fail to strengthen your faith and renew your purpose.

40.   Man may come into full harmony with the Formless Substance by entertaining a lively and sincere gratitude for the blessings it bestows upon him. Gratitude unifies the mind of man with the intelligence of Substance, so that man's thoughts are received by the Formless.

41.   Man must form a clear and definite mental image of the things he wishes to have, to do, or to become; and he must hold this mental image in his thoughts, while being deeply grateful to the Supreme that all his desires are granted to him. The man who wishes to get rich must spend his leisure hours in contemplating his Vision, and in earnest thanksgiving that the reality is being given to him.

42.   Too much stress cannot be laid on the importance of frequent contemplation of the mental image, coupled with unwavering faith and devout gratitude. This is the process by

which the impression is given to the Formless, and the creative forces set in motion.

43.   The whole matter turns on receiving, once you have clearly formed your vision. When you have formed it, it is well to make an oral statement, addressing the Supreme in reverent prayer; and from that moment you must, in mind, receive what you ask for.

44.   In order to receive his own when it shall come to him, man must be active And he must do, every day, all that can be done that day, taking care to do each act in a successful manner and he must so hold the Advancing Thought that the impression of increase will be communicated to all with whom he comes in contact.

- *There is a thinking substance from which all things are made, and which, in its original state, permeates, penetrates, and fills the interspaces of the universe.*

- *A thought, sent into this substance, Produces the thing that is imaged by the thought.*

- *Man can form things in his thought, and, by impressing his thought upon formless substance, can cause the thing he thinks about to be created.*

- *In order to do this, man must pass from the competitive to the creative mind; he must form a clear mental picture of the things he wants, and hold this picture in his thoughts with the fixed PURPOSE to get what he wants, and the unwavering FAITH that he does get what he wants, closing his mind to all that may tend to shake his purpose, dim his vision, or quench his faith.*

- *That he may receive what he wants when it comes, man must act NOW upon the people and things in his present environment.*

- *In order to do this, man must pass from the competitive to the creative mind; he must form a clear mental picture of the things he wants, and do, with faith and purpose, all that can be done each day, doing each separate thing in an efficient manner.*

- Man may come into full harmony with the Formless Substance by entertaining a lively and sincere gratitude for the blessings it bestows upon him. Gratitude unifies the mind of man with the intelligence of Substance, so that man's thoughts are received by the Formless.

- Man must form a clear and definite mental image of the things he wishes to have, to do, or to become; and he must hold this mental image in his thoughts, while being deeply grateful to the Supreme that all his desires are granted to him. The man who wishes to get rich must spend his leisure hours in contemplating his Vision, and in earnest thanksgiving that the reality is being given to him.

- In order to receive his own when it shall come to him, man must be active; and this activity can only consist in more than filling his present place. He must keep in mind the Purpose to get rich through the realization of his mental image. And he must do, every day, all that can be done that day, taking care to do each act in a successful manner. He must give to every man a use value in excess of the cash value he receives, so that each transaction makes for more life; and he must so hold the Advancing Thought that the impression of increase will be communicated to all with whom he comes in contact. [i]

Quotes on Prosperity and Abundance

- **"Wealth is not his that has it, but his who enjoys it." — Benjamin Franklin**

- **"Life is a field of unlimited possibilities." —Deepak Chopra**

- **"He who is plenteously provided for from within, needs but little from without." —Johann Wolfgang von Goethe**

- **"Take full account of the excellencies which you possess, and in gratitude remember how you would hanker after them, if you had them not." —Marcus Aurelius**

- "Whenever anything negative happens to you, there is a deep lesson concealed within it, although you may not see it at the time." —Eckhart Tolle

- "If you want to change who you are, begin by changing the size of your dream. Even if you are broke, it does not cost you anything to dream of being rich. Many poor people are poor because they have given up on dreaming." —Robert Kiyosaki

- "Ideas are the beginning points of all fortunes." —Napoleon Hill

- "When you are grateful fear disappears and abundance appears." —Anthony Robbins

"Everything in the universe has a purpose. Indeed, the invisible intelligence that flows through everything in a purposeful fashion is also flowing through you." —Dr. Wayne Dyer

- "Gratitude is an attitude that hooks us up to our source of supply. And the more grateful you are, the closer you become to your maker, to the architect of the universe, to the spiritual core of your being. It's a phenomenal lesson." —Bob Proctor

- "Living in Abundance and Success is a Reasonable Option" — Magus Incognito

- "You have a divine right to abundance, and if you are anything less than a millionaire, you haven't had your fair share." — Stuart Wilde

- "Prosperity is not just having things. It is the consciousness that attracts the things. Prosperity is a way of living and thinking, and not just having money or things. Poverty is a way of living and thinking, and not just a lack of money or things." —Eric Butterworth

- "Most folks are about as happy as they make up their minds to be." —Abraham Lincoln

- *"And he shall be like a tree planted by the rivers of water, that bringeth forth his fruit in his season; his leaf also shall not wither; and whatsoever he doeth shall prosper."* —Psalm 1:3

- "The Constitution only gives people the right to pursue happiness. You have to catch it yourself." —Benjamin Franklin

- "Not what we have But what we enjoy, constitutes our abundance." — Epicurus

- "Gratitude is the vital ingredient in the recipe for Faith" — Magus Incognito

- "We may divide thinkers into those who think for themselves and those who think through others. The latter are the rule and the former the exception. The first are original thinkers in a double sense, and egotists in the noblest meaning of the word." —Arthur Schopenhauer

- "The key to every man is his thought. Sturdy and defiant though he look he has a helm which he obeys, which is the idea after which all his facts are classified. He can only be reformed by showing him a new idea which commands his own." —Ralph Waldo Emerson

- "All truly wise thoughts have been thought already thousands of times; but to make them really ours we must think them over again honestly till they take root in our personal expression." — Johann Wolfgang von Goethe.

- "Great men are they who see that spirituality is stronger than any material force; that thoughts rule the world." —Ralph Waldo Emerson.

- "All that we are is a result of what we have thought." —Buddha

- "Wealth is the slave of a wise man. The master of a fool." — Seneca

- "Happiness is not in the mere possession of money; it lies in the joy of achievement, in the thrill of creative effort." — Franklin D Roosevelt

- "Money is like manure. You have to spread it around or it smells." — J. Paul Getty

- "Liberty is not a means to a higher political end. It is the highest political end." — Lord John Dalberg-Acton

- "We are what we repeatedly do. Excellence, then, is not an act but a habit." —Aristotle

- "Money is like love; it kills slowly and painfully the one who withholds it, and enlivens the other who turns it on his fellow man." — Kahlil Gibran

- "Empty pockets never held anyone back. Only empty heads and empty hearts can do that." —Norman Vincent Peale

- "The thief cometh not, but for to steal, and to kill, and to destroy: I am come that they might have life, and that they might have it more abundantly." —John 10:10, KJV

- "Prosperity is not without many fears and distastes, and adversity is not without comforts and hopes." —Francis Bacon

- "It is health that is real wealth and not pieces of gold and silver." — Mahatma Gandhi

- "Desire is the starting point of all achievement, not a hope, not a wish, but a keen pulsating desire, which transcends everything. When your desires are strong enough you will appear to possess superhuman powers to achieve."— Napoleon Hill

- "Move out of your comfort zone. You can only grow if you are willing to feel awkward and uncomfortable when you try something new." — Brian Tracy

- "You can open your mind to prosperity when you realize the true definition of the word: You are prosperous to the degree you are experiencing peace, health and plenty in your world." —Catherine Ponder, *Open Your Mind to Prosperity*

• "There is a science of getting rich and it is an exact science, like algebra or arithmetic. There are certain laws which govern the process of acquiring riches and once these laws are learned and obeyed by anyone, that person will get rich with mathematical certainty." —*Wallace D. Wattles*

• "Within you right now is the power to do things you never dreamed possible. This power becomes available to you just as soon as you can change your beliefs." —*Dr. Maxwell Maltz*

Summary of Ideas – A Parabolic Workbook to Success

About the Author George Mentz –

Commissioner George Mentz JD MBA CWM <u>Chartered Wealth Manager</u> ® is an international book award winning author, award winning professor, licensed attorney and CEO of GAFM ® global education. Mentz has been recognized as the #2 in the world as a Wealth Management influencer and his Wealth Management Handbook has reached the top 75 Wealth books in History. Mentz's education companies are ISO 21001 and ISO 9001 Certified professional development companies offering <u>wealth management</u> training & operating in over 50 nations. Mentz is an advisory board member to several companies around the world in education, charities, and FinTech Companies. Mentz holds a Doctor of Jurisprudence degree, and MBA, and a Graduate International Law Diploma/Certificate along with federal and state law licenses. Mentz is an Associate of The St. George's House, Windsor Castle, UK. Mentz and his companies have been seen in The Hill, The Wall Street Journal, The Week UK, The Hindu, the El Norte Mexico, <u>Magazine of Wall Street</u>, Newsmax, The China Daily, ABC,NBC, CBS, FOX, The Arab Times, and many more. Mentz is the titular Lord/Seigneur of the Fief Blondel Est. 1270 AD and the titular Lord of Eynerdale in Cumbria UK. All Rights Reserved 2021

Other References or Authors of Interest

Allen, J. (1998). *As You Think*. Edited with an introduction by M. Allen. Novato, CA: New World Library.

Aurelius, M. (1964) *Meditations*, trans. M. Staniforth, London: Penguin.

The Bhagavad-Gita (1973) trans. J. Mascaró, London: Penguin World's Classics..

Behrend, G. (1927) *Your Invisible Power*. Montana: Kessinger Publishing.

Carnegie, D. (1994). *How to Win Friends and Influence People*. New York: Pocket Books.

Carlson, R. (2001). *Don't Sweat the Small Stuff About Money*. New York, USA: Hyperion.

Chopra, D. (1996). *The Seven Spiritual Laws of Success*. London: Bantam Press.

Collier, R. (1970). *Be Rich*. Oak Harbor, Washington: Robert Collier Publishing.

Coelho, P. (1999) *The Alchemist*, trans. Alan R Clarke, London: HarperCollins.

Covey, S. R. (1989). *The 7 Habits of Highly Effective People*. London: Simon & Schuster.

Dyer, W. (1993). *Real Magic: Creating Miracles in Everyday Life*. New York: HarperCollins.

Eker, T. H. (2005). *Secrets of the Millionaire Mind: Mastering the Inner Game of Wealth*. New York: HarperCollins Publishers.

Emerson, R.W. (1993) *Self-Reliance*, Dover Publications.

Gawain, Shakti (1979). *Creative Visualization*. New World Library, Mill Valley USA.

Bishop Bernard Jordan (2007). The Laws of Thinking: 20 Secrets to Using the Divine Power of Your Mind to Manifest Prosperity." (2007) *(9781401917968): Published by Hay House and Bishop E. Bernard Jordan: Books*

Hill, N. (1960). *Think and Grow Rich.* New York: Fawcett Crest.

His Holiness the Dalai Lama, with H. C. Cutler (1999). *The Art of Happiness: A Handbook for Living.* London: Hodder & Stroughton.

James, W. (1902). *The Varieties of Religious Experience.* Longman Publishing, London, UK.

Jeffers, S. (1991) Feel the Fear and Do It Anyway, London: Arrow Books.

Lao-Tzu's Tao Te Ching (2000) trans. T. Freke, introduction by M.

Palmer, London: Piatkus.

Maltz, M.. (1960). *Psycho-Cybernetics.* New York. Pocket Books.

Marden, O. S. (1997). *Pushing to the Front, or Success under Difficulties,* Vols. 1–2. Santa Fe, California: Sun Books.

Mentz, C. W. H. (2007). *Masters of the Secrets: And the Science of Getting Rich and Master Key System Expanded: Bestseller Version.* Bloomington, Indiana, United States: Xlibris Corp.

Mentz, C. W. H. (2006). *How to Master Abundance and Prosperity— The Master Key System Decoded.* Bloomington Indiana: Xlibris Pub.

Mentz, C. W. H. (2005). *The Science of Growing Rich.* Bloomington, Indiana: Xlibris Publishing.

Mentz, George S - *Other Books by Mentz.*
http://www.lulu.com/gmentz

Mulford, P. (1908). *Thoughts Are Things: Essays Selected from the White Cross Library.* G. Bell and Sons, Ltd., LONDON, 1908.

Murphy, J. (1963). *The Power of Your Subconscious Mind.* New Jersey: Prentice Hall.

Peale, N.V. (1996) *The Power of Positive Thinking,* New York: Ballantine Books.

Ponder, C. (1962). *The Dynamic Laws of Prosperity.* Camarillo, California: DeVorss & Co.

Price, J. R. (1987). *The Abundance Book.* Carlsbad, California: Hay House.

Roman, S., Packer, D. R. (2008). Creating Money: *Attracting Abundance*. Tiburon, California: H. J. Kramer, Inc., published in a joint venture with New World Library.

Scovell Shinn, F. (1998) *The Game of Life and How to Play It*, Saffron

Walden: C.W. Daniel.

Seicho-no Iye (生長の家). Books by Dr. Masaharu Taniguchi.

Smiles, S. (2002). *Self-Help: With Illustrations of Character, Conduct, and Perseverance*. Oxford: Oxford University Press.

Thoreau, H.D. (1986) *Walden and Civil Disobedience*, introduction by M. Meyer, New York: Penguin.

Tracy, B. (1993). *Maximum Achievement: Strategies and Skills That Will Unlock Your Hidden Powers to Succeed*. New York: Fireside.

Troward, T. (1904). *The Edinburgh Lectures on Mental Science*. DODD, MEAD & COMPANY: New York.

Wattles, W. D. (1976). *Financial Success through the Power of Thought: The Science of Getting Rich*. Rochester, Vermont: Destiny Books.

Wilkinson, B. (2000). *The Prayer of Jabez*. Colorado Springs, CO USA, OR: Multnamah Publishers.

---

[i] Wattles, W. D. (1976). *Financial Success through the Power of Thought: The Science of Getting Rich*. Rochester, Vermont: Destiny Books.